4.99

object TALKS That Teach the Gospels

25 Lessons for Elementary Kids

Zach Hapeman

STANDARD PUBLISHING
Cincinnati, Ohio

To every child
who has marched to the front pew
with faith unhindered,
a hope unbound.

The Standard Publishing Company, Cincinnati, Ohio
A division of Standex International Corporation.
Copyright© 1999 by Zach Hapeman.
All rights reserved. Printed in United States of America.

06 05 04 03 02 01 00 99   5 4 3 2 1

ISBN 0-7847-0941-6

Illustrations by Rusty Fletcher
Cover design by Sandi Welch

Contents

Introduction

If you were dropped into a foreign mission field and could choose to take only one book of the Bible with you, which one would it be? If you could take only one chapter of a book, one verse, which would those be? Thankfully, we don't have to limit ourselves that way in ministry, but if I had to choose only one book, I'm sure it would be one of the Gospels.

I would take one of the Gospels because as I work with children nothing seems more important than letting them know that God so loved the world. Nothing is more crucial than telling them about the one with whom God was so pleased. As I get to know and love these children, nothing is more urgent than introducing them to the one who has set me free, the one who really invites them forward every Sunday morning.

Jesus Christ is what ministry is all about, and the Gospels are all about him. Matthew, Mark, Luke and John, no other books are so effective in describing the heart of our Lord, the heart of God, and no other books provide as perfect an introduction to the one who makes us complete.

This book of stories is based upon the Gospels, but more importantly, it is based upon the life of love—the words and actions of Jesus Christ. And if anyone can minister to children, he can.

Walk like an Egyptian

THEME: Despite the numerous ways to walk in life, God wants us to walk like Jesus.

SUPPLIES: A cane or walker, gumption.

POINT: The demonstration of a variety of walks will lead to the point of "walking" as Jesus did.

Have you ever noticed that different people have different types of walks? Have you ever seen someone walk like this? *(Walk on your tiptoes.)*

That's someone trying to be quiet, isn't it? Well, have you ever seen someone walk like this? *(Use the cane or walker to imitate a limp or injury.)*

That's how someone walks if he has hurt his leg. How about like this? *(Walk like an Egyptian.)*

Have you ever seen anyone walk like that? Would you like to try a walk? How about this? *(Walk with a big strut, stop to hike up your belt, and snort like a lumberjack.)*

Have you ever seen a walk like that? OK, stand up and walk like this. *(Crouch down, flap your wings, stick out your tail feathers and bob your head like a chicken.)*

You'd look pretty silly walking around like that, wouldn't you?

Well, let me ask you a question: You can walk like all sorts of people, and even chickens, but do you know how to walk like Jesus? *(They may have a silly suggestion and they may even want to demonstrate. Go ahead and let them do it but remember to point out that they're just being silly.)*

Have any of you seen Jesus walk? One of the things God wants us to do in this life is to walk as Jesus walked.

But how are we going to walk like Jesus if we haven't seen him walking?

This is kind of a trick question because when God tells us that we must walk as Jesus walked (1 John 2:6), he means that we must live as Jesus lived. In other words, God wants us to obey his commandments and try to live a perfect, sinless life.

That's a very difficult walk to take, but God has given us some instruction on how we can walk more like Jesus in the Bible. The Bible describes the events of Jesus' life and all of God's commandments so that we can understand how God wants us to live. God doesn't really want us to "walk" like Jesus did, copying the motion of Jesus' body, he wants us to live like Jesus, loving others and praising and obeying God. Now let me see you walk like Jesus.

John 17:11, 15

Sinburn and Sonscreen

THEME: Jesus Christ is our only Savior from the punishment of sin.
SUPPLIES: Sunscreen, sunglasses, really tacky Hawaiian shirt, flip-flops (anything that is summer/beach oriented).
POINT: What type of UV protection do we need to prevent our obliteration in God's perfect, sinless light? We need JC level 1. Christ is central to our salvation; just like sunscreen and sunshine, we need to be covered by the blood of Jesus to save us from the cost of sin.

How many of you like the sun? Do you like going to the beach and playing in the warm light? Me too.

You know, some days I could stay out in the sun all day long. I would like to stay in the sun forever. But I can't. You know why? Right, sunburn!

The sun is a great thing but it can be very dangerous if we don't protect ourselves, and as much as we love the sun, we really can't be in the sun for very long without getting burned. Now how would we keep ourselves safe from the sunlight? Right, sunscreen.

What else could we use to keep the sun off? Right, an umbrella, or a hat, or sunglasses. All of these things enable us to stay out in the sun longer. On a sunny day, I wouldn't want to be without my sunscreen and hat.

You know, God and the sun are a lot alike. God is a perfect being. He has absolutely no sin. In fact, you all know that sin offends God. Sin is something that God has told us he will not tolerate because he *cannot* tolerate it. Sin cannot exist in God's presence. His perfection will burn sin up. Now this poses a bit of a problem for all of us, doesn't it?

Yes, we're all sinners. We have a hard time not sinning. We lie, cheat, say mean things, think we're the best, hate other people, envy others, etc. We are all sinners. But God still loves us. He has told us over and over that he loves us and God doesn't lie.

I love God too, and I want to be resting in his warm presence, just like I want to lie out in the sun but I can't. God is like the sun because his perfection burns up our sin. None of us can enter into God's presence because we have sin in our lives.

Now how can we enter into God's awesome light without getting burned up by it? With Jesus! Jesus is like our sunscreen, he's our sun hat, our umbrella, his perfect life covers our sins. He died so that we can be with God even though we are sinners. If you have Jesus in your life, you don't have to worry about your sin causing you to get burned in God's perfect presence.

You know, on any day, I wouldn't want to be without Jesus.

John 1:9-12

Come and Get It

THEME: Before any of us have anything worth giving, we have to receive Jesus.

SUPPLIES: Enough jelly beans to share with all the kids.

POINT: Tell the children that you have something for them, something that they'll really love. Tell them it's theirs if they want it. You've got enough for anyone who wants to have it. Chances are the kids aren't going to be brave enough to jump up right away and ask you for what you have. Eventually, however, after they realize that you aren't going to place it in their hands, they'll understand that they have to step forward and receive what you have for them. God works the same way. He's given us Christ as a gift, but we have to receive God's gift before we'll have it. Make sense?

I sure do appreciate your coming to spend time with me. I love seeing your happy faces, and I love being with you. Because you are all so special to me, I've brought something special just for you. It's all yours, and I want you to have it.

(Pour it on thick, but keep the goodies in your pocket.)

It's something really good. Wow, you are really going to love this. I can't wait until you get it, and the good news is, there's enough for absolutely everyone who wants some of it.

(Things should be getting a little awkward now. But stand there in silence with a smile and wait until one of the children gets brave enough to come to you and ask for what you have brought for them. Then give that child a treat and try to stay on your feet as the rest of the children charge forward.)

I'm so glad you came to receive what I had for you. You know, God works the same way. He has provided something really sweet for us, better than simple jelly beans. God has given us his Son. When Jesus died on the cross, he became a gift for us. He was punished for all of the bad things we do, and we were forgiven by God. But we can't have that gift unless we go to Jesus and ask him for it. God wants us to have forgiveness so much, he has provided it free for us. But it doesn't automatically appear in our pockets; we have to go and take it. We do that by asking Jesus to become the Lord of our lives and apologizing for all our sin.

You've heard the saying, "It's better to give than to receive." Well, how much better it is to receive in this case. Let's pray and thank God for the gift of Jesus.

Luke 1:52

Invisible Touch

THEME: God supports his children.
SUPPLIES: Balsam wood airplane (These planes can be found at most discount stores. Don't put one together until you do the story).
POINT: The frail pieces of balsam are broken and shaped into a plane. The plane appears to fly but it is actually supported by the air in the room. Christians are the same—frail and shaped by God into something that is lifted up by his supporting strength.

Do you know what type of wood this is? (*Show them the plane unassembled.*) This is called balsam wood and it's very fragile. (*Break a tiny piece off of the body of the plane.*)

It's easy to hurt this wood, and you wouldn't think the wood was any good being this weak, but let me show you something. *(Assemble the plane.)*

This wood is very special because of what it can do. Now watch this. *(Throw the plane and ask whoever gets it to hold it until you ask that it be thrown back.)*

Even though this wood is very weak, it can float through the air. The plane doesn't really fly, it's actually being supported by the air. Like invisible hands, the air in the room is lifting up the plane and holding it until it gently reaches the ground. *(Ask the plane holder to throw the plane back.)* People are a lot like this plane. We're very weak and we can be hurt easily, but God has promised us that he will hold us in his arms and lift us up safely to new heights. Now we can't see God's hands, but we know they're there; just like we can't see the air, but we know it's all around us. Would you like to see the plane fly once more? *(If they ask to throw it, tell them they can throw it after the service is over.)* Let's thank God for holding us safely in his hands. *(Pray.)*

Matthew 11:28-30

Silent Pictures

THEME: God can fix the broken you.
SUPPLIES: Two identical photos of yourself, a marker, a cross, a box big enough to hold it all.
POINT: No words are spoken in this presentation. The lesson of God's desire for us is told only through the props provided and gestures. The point is that while we are sinners, destroying ourselves, God still loves us and can make us whole again. The point is illustrated through a photo's destruction and apparent restoration.

Once all the children are seated, settle them with the "silence" gesture, shhhhh. Get them to "shhhhh" with you. Then point to your eyes and get them to point to their eyes. Try to communicate the idea that you want them to watch very closely what you're going to share with them. Once they get the idea, show them one of the pictures of you. Smile and pass it around. Treat it roughly. Don't be afraid to fold the corners, wrinkle the edges, even tear it here and there.

Once you get it back, pull out your marker and draw a mustache on your picture. Show the kids your artistry and continue with the defacement. Try some new glasses, pimples, a beard and big ears. Laugh silently, acting as though this is the greatest fun. Gradually let your enjoyment dwindle and then try to rub off your sketching with your thumb. It won't work but keep trying, gradually increasing your frustration and anxiety. Eventually, let the picture be ripped apart by your anxious fingers and then tenderly hold the pieces of your picture with a look of despair. The idea you are trying to communicate is that you've destroyed something very precious to you.

Then act like you hear something. Turn your head and look up, like what you're hearing is coming from God. Look back to the box that you so strategically placed earlier and then back to him. Point upwards, then at the box, and then puzzlingly point to yourself, as if to say, "For me?" Go to the box, open it and pull out the cross. Treat it with all the wonder and respect it deserves. Hold it tentatively in your hands and then bring it right to your heart in a gesture of thanks.

Hold on. God is saying more. Look upwards as though you're listening and then slowly look down at your damaged picture. Shake your head and hold the picture with just two fingers as if to say, "No, God, you wouldn't want this. It's all tattered and ugly." Then, shrugging, put the picture in the box and return to the fascination you had with the cross.

(Here is where things get interesting. The children don't know that you've got a duplicate picture hidden behind one of the box flaps, so the children can see into the box and think it is empty except for the cross.)

Once more, look upwards as though God were speaking to you. Look to the box and point to yourself again asking, "For me?" Open the box and pull out the second picture of you, brand new and unwrinkled. You are trying to create the illusion that this is the old picture restored. Act reasonably astonished, and look from the picture to the cross. One last time, look up at God who is speaking to you. Act as though he is saying, "Spread the cross around." Nod OK and pass it to one of the children, encouraging her to pass it along to the other kids.

Once all the kids have held the cross, get up and begin to leave the room. Pause halfway as though you've forgotten something. Turn back to the box and your picture (left outside of the box). Pick up the photo and look up again. Put the picture in the box and set the box on the table or floor and continue out of the room.

John 3:16

Watch your language

THEME: God expressed his love for us by sacrificing his only Son. Jesus said, "I love you," by dying.

SUPPLIES: A sign language dictionary (check out the local library).

POINT: Kids will learn how difficult it is to communicate without using words, but they'll understand the significance of Christ's wordless sacrifice.

Language is such a neat thing, isn't it? Language is the way we communicate with others. What types of languages can you think of? English, French, Spanish, Portuguese, Greek. How about body language or sign language?

(Show the children your sign language dictionary. Open it up and let them see the illustrations inside.)

This is a book of sign language. Sign language is a way to talk using just your hands. People who have trouble hearing or speaking can use sign language to communicate with each other.

(If you have the time to prepare, demonstrate a few signed words or letters from the book.)

There are all kinds of languages that people use to let others know their thoughts and feelings. Now, I want to try a little experiment with you.

Let's imagine that none of you can speak. Let's imagine that we have no verbal language to speak to others and we don't know any sign language. I'm going to give each of you an assignment. I'm going to tell you what you need to say to me but you can't use any words to do it. For example, I might ask you to tell me that your hair is on fire, and you would tell me without speaking. OK? All right, here we go:

Hello.

I'm hungry.

Help me, I'm choking.

My back is sore.

There's a spider on your shirt!

Excuse me, Sir, but you're standing on my foot.

Hooray!

I love you.

Very good; you all did terrific.

You know, Jesus told us something very important without using any words. It's kind of funny really because Jesus is known as the Word of God, but the most important thing he's ever said to us didn't require any words. Jesus showed us he loved us without using any words at all. His demonstration of love was communicated through an action, through something he did. You see, Jesus died for us. He did something that no one else would ever do, he gave up his life for us. That's one way we know he loves us, because he gave up his life so that we could enter God's glory in heaven. That's a pretty incredible way to say, "I love you," isn't it? That's something to be thankful about too. *(Read John 3:16.)*

Mark 6:35-44

Pennies From Heaven

THEME: God can turn our poverty into riches if we trust him to.
SUPPLIES: As many pennies as you can find, and a Bible.
POINT: When we add as the world does, our increases are what we'd expect, but when we put God into the equation, the old math goes out the window.

(Keep seven pennies in your pocket and put the rest in your sleeve just before you do the story. Keep your Bible in the hand whose sleeve holds all the pennies and keep your elbow bent so the pennies don't fall out. If you hold your Bible close to your chest it will look pretty natural and no one will suspect the pennies.)

Have you children heard about the miracle when Jesus feeds thousands of people with only five loaves of bread and two fish? That must have been incredible to see, don't you think? But really, that's just an example of how God can turn nothing into something.

Do you know how to add yet? *(Show the children your seven pennies in a group of five and two, for the loaves and fish.)* Well, if we add these pennies up the way the world does, then we end up with seven. Five plus two equals seven.

But I think God does math differently. When we add God to any equation, he can take away our sorrow and add great joy—far more joy than we expected. God really multiplies the results beyond our expectations.

Let me show you. Five, plus two, plus God equals . . . *(Quickly place your Bible down straightening your arm and letting the change pour out of your sleeve. If you do it quickly enough, the change will seem to appear out of nowhere).*

Did you know that God has provided for all our needs through Jesus Christ? Because Jesus died on the cross, we have the chance to become heirs to all the riches of heaven. All we have to do is choose Jesus over everything else in the world, making him the one we love most in our lives.

Matthew 4:19

Whistlin' Fisherman

THEME: In order to be "fishers of men," we have to be using the right type of bait.

SUPPLIES: Fishing pole (a stick and some string will do), Bible, a fishing hole (maybe a box or a covered table), gum, a balloon, a pair of rubber boots, a sock, a hat, a comb or brush, and a helper.

POINT: You're fishing, and each item you use as bait catches you something related to the bait. When you use the Bible as bait, you'll pull in your helper.

(Set up your fishing hole beforehand with all the big ones you're going to pull out of it. This story requires no speaking but does require a helper.)

The whistlin' fisherman comes in chewing his gum and wearing a hat and only one boot. He takes a seat, throws his line in the fishing hole and whistles. Finally the fisherman pulls his line out and examines the end. Realizing there is no bait, he looks for something to use. Having nothing around he takes his gum, sticks it on the end of the line, chucks it back in the hole and starts whistling. Suddenly he gets a few tugs on the rod. He imitates the jerks and pulls of reeling in a fish and then pulls out an inflated balloon on the end of his line. Whistling with surprise, he pulls it off his line and looks for something else to use as bait.

Aha! his sock. He takes off his sock, smells it and lets out a long whistle of disgust. He ties the sock to the line *(a slipknot works very well with all the transferring of bait and catches)*, chucks it in and continues to whistle. Repeating the process above, he pulls out a boot. Just what he needed, now he has two boots.

He takes off his hat and rustles his hair with his handkerchief as if it were a really hot day. Oh no, messy hair. He tries to fix his hair with his hands, but discovering it to be a futile endeavor, he plucks a hair and attaches it to the line. This time he pulls out a brush, brushes his hair and whistles.

Finally, he searches for one last item to use as bait and happens upon the Bible. He opens it up and reads to himself while whistling "Jesus Loves Me." Deciding the Bible would make some good bait, he puts it on his line and casts it into the hole. This time the struggle is more intense, the fisherman has got a big one on the line. After a few moments of wild tugging and jerking, up pops the helper from the hole with the line in her mouth and the Bible in her hands. The fisherman lets out a long whistle of surprise and helps the helper out of the hole. Once out of the hole, she reads Matthew 4:19 aloud.

Mark 16:1

Empty Easter

THEME: Easter is about celebrating Christ's resurrection.
SUPPLIES: Enough plastic eggs for everyone.
POINT: The children will expect your egg to be full of treats, just like every other egg they find this Easter. When they, disappointedly, find their eggs are empty, they can be reminded of the joy Jesus' friends had in realizing that the empty tomb they found meant Jesus was alive.

(Distribute the eggs and tell the children not to open them until you tell them they may).

What's special about today? It's Easter! Today we celebrate Jesus' resurrection by finding all kinds of goodies around the house. Now you know what this is *(hold up your egg)*. And what do you think is inside of the egg? Candy, right! On Easter we look for eggs like this one that we can open up and find all kinds of sweet loveliness inside.

OK, open up your eggs.

Hey! This isn't right. These eggs are empty. This is nothing to get excited about. This doesn't make you want to shout for joy and go tell all of your friends what you found, does it? In fact, you're probably thinking that someone stole what was in your egg.

Well, let me tell you something. I gave you empty eggs on purpose because today we should be celebrating a discovery of nothing. We should be overjoyed at finding emptiness. Because this day represents the day that Jesus' friends went to look for his body after he had been crucified.

Jesus' friends went to a place called a tomb to find his

body. That tomb was a cave covered by a large stone. The cave was kind of like an egg. And when Jesus' friends opened that tomb—when they rolled back the stone—they found nothing. Jesus' body wasn't there, the tomb was empty.

And do you know what they did? They did the same thing we'd do with an empty egg. They thought somebody had come by and stolen Jesus' body. They were looking around saying, "Who stole the body from this tomb." It wasn't until later that they realized that nobody had stolen Jesus—he had come back to life. He had risen from the dead and left the tomb empty.

This made them really happy. It's a happiness that we share too. We can rejoice in the empty tomb because it means that Jesus beat death and through him we will beat death too.

While you look for all the full eggs today, remember the empty one and the good news that we're reminded of by the empty tomb.

Matthew 5:12

God Is Like Donuts

THEME: When we only see the bad in life, it's because we have forgotten how much greater the good is.

SUPPLIES: At least two donuts of varying sizes. Most grocery stores carry small sugar donuts that can be dwarfed by any donut from a donut shop.

POINT: Compare the holes in two donuts. The bigger the hole; the bigger the donut. Same way with God. When we are focused on what's missing in our lives and the troubles we bear, we often forget what's not missing. God is like donuts because the more difficulty we have, the more present he is. The bigger the hole in our lives; the bigger the donut God holds out for us.

Do you ever feel like nothing is going your way, like the whole world is out to get you? Have you ever had a bad day? Have you ever gotten up in the morning and just felt like being blue, kind of sad?

I think it's easy for us to look more at the bad things in our lives than the good things. We always notice the bad things that happen to us. We always notice when we hurt ourselves or lose a favorite toy, or when we get into an argument with a friend. But we don't always notice the good things in our lives, like the fact that God, the creator of the universe, has a special place in his heart just for us.

The Bible tells us that because God loves us so much, he has created a great reward for us in heaven. So we should rejoice and be glad, not glum and full of sadness.

We have the biggest, best, most powerful and awesome person on our side—God. How often when we're feeling bad do we forget that?

I think that God is like donuts. *(Pull out a small donut.)* We are always looking at the hole, saying, "I wish I had more of this," and "I never have anything good happen to me." But the whole time we look at the hole, we forget about everything that is around that hole: all the blessings God has given us in our families, our friends, our health and best of all, our Savior Jesus Christ and the reward we have in heaven.

Now that's all fine and good, but here is the best thing about having God in our lives: *(pull out a big donut)* the bigger the hole, the more donut there is to be thankful for. We forget that as God's children, he is blessing and protecting us even more when times are bad. When we're feeling like the whole world is crashing down, that's when God really gets close and says: "Rejoice and be glad because great is your reward in heaven."

Matthew 22:37

Children's Children's Story

THEME: God wants all parts of our being to love him.
SUPPLIES: A loaf of bread, a carton of milk, a stick of butter, a pen, paper, the story template (below), and actors (optional).
POINT: The boy who didn't buy all of his mother's requests at the grocery store has disappointed her. Likewise, God wants us to love him with all parts of our being, not just one. The children's contributions to this story make for some good fun and will cause the story's lesson to leave a lasting impression.

Good morning, boys and girls. I have a question for you: Why is the children's story never told by the children? I mean it is the children's story, right? That's what people call it. But you never tell the story. Well today, that's going to change. Today, you are going to create your very own children's story.

Now I need you to give me your ideas for important parts of the story, so I need to ask you a few questions. *(Ask the children for one of each of the following items. Write down their responses so you don't forget them.)*

1) A boy's name
2) A topping put on ice cream
3) A vegetable
4) A number between 1 and 100

(Use the following story by inserting the children's suggestions for the above items into the corresponding numbered spaces. Place the bread, milk and butter on a table

or chair as though they were on display in a store. Prompt your actors as you need to, or, if you aren't using actors, emphasize the bread, milk and butter as they are mentioned.)

One fine day, a boy named (1) was going to the grocery store for his mother. She had given him (4) dollars and asked him to buy three things: a loaf of bread, a carton of milk and a stick of butter.

When (1) got to the store, he saw a beautiful (2) covered (3) in the window. *(Make this imaginary treat seem absolutely marvelous, either through your actors or your own facial expressions.)* Oh, how he loved a good (2) covered (3). (1) counted the (4) dollars he had. He didn't have enough money to get everything his mother asked for and that wonderful (2) covered (3). But (1) did have enough money for just two of his mother's things plus the delicious treat.

(1) thought to himself: "Maybe Mom won't mind if I just get two of the things she asked for; she knows how much I love a sweet (2) covered (3)."

So that's what (1) did. And he returned home with a loaf of bread and a carton of milk but no stick of butter. *(Ask your actors to freeze or be seated at this point.)*

Do you think when (1) got home his mother was happy? No, she wasn't happy, was she? Why wasn't she happy? Right, because (1) did only part of what she asked.

Did you know that God has asked us to love him with three things? Jesus said: *(Read aloud Matthew 22:37.)* He wants us to love him with all that we are, not just one part, or two parts, but with our hearts *(point to the bread)* and souls *(point to the milk)* and minds *(point to the butter)* —with all of our parts. Do you think God would be happy if he asked us to love him with three things and we loved him with only two? No, he wants us to love him with everything we have.

You know, you tell a really good story. Now let's ask for God's help in loving him properly. *(Pray.)*

Matthew 5:14-16

Hot Wax and Candle-shine

THEME: We need to share the light of Jesus with others.
SUPPLIES: Three candles and some matches.
POINT: The light of the candles represents Jesus, but in order for other candles to catch fire, they must be contacted by a lit candle.

(You're going to need two people to each hold one of your extra candles. If you feel comfortable enough doing so, choose two of your children, but watch them carefully once their candles are lit.)

The Bible tells us that Jesus is like a light unto the world and that his light gives light to everyone (John 1:9). When we invite Jesus into our lives, he makes our hearts shine like this candle. *(Light your candle.)*

God wants everyone to have the forgiveness Jesus gives, and he wants all of us to shine like a light. But people need to see the light of Jesus in us so that they will know God is so good.

These candles cannot be lit unless they come into contact with one that is lit. *(Light one of the other candles with your own.)* Unless the light of a candle is shared with another, the other won't catch fire. *(Help the holder of the newly lit candle light the remaining candle.)* That's how Jesus spreads to other people; he is passed on by people like us who have him shining in our hearts. We have to share Jesus with others. Let's pray and ask God to help us share Jesus. *(Pray.)*

luke 2:10, 11

upside-down Christmas

THEME: Christ is at the heart of Christmas.

SUPPLIES: A candy cane (if you have the means, get enough candy canes for all the kids).

POINT: A candy cane is usually hung on a tree, but the significance of Christmas can be seen when the canes are held upside down. Their "J" shape reminds us of Jesus and the joy he brings us.

Who knows what this is? *(Hold up the candy cane.)* Right, it's a candy cane. Do any of you have these hanging on your Christmas tree at home? Its shape makes it perfect for hanging on things, doesn't it?

You know, to tell you the truth, I sometimes laugh at a tree that has candy canes hanging on it. I think it's funny and I have to laugh because most people hang their candy canes wrong.

Let me explain: What does this shape mean to you? *(Hold up your candy cane in the conventional curve-on-the-top manner.)* Nothing, right? But if you flip it over, what have you got then? *(Turn your candy cane over into the "J" position.)* It's a "J." That reminds me of what's important about Christmas—Jesus. The name *Jesus* starts with the letter "J."

When we put up our tree and hang lights on the house and spend hours in a crowded shopping mall buying presents and eating goodies, we can sometimes forget what Christmastime is all about. It's about Jesus. We celebrate this time of year because it's Jesus' birthday, the day God sent love to earth.

Jesus was God's gift to us; he is the gift of life because

through him we are freed from sin and death.

That's some kind of Christmas present, isn't it? That's the kind of present that makes me want to jump for joy.

So the next time you see a tree with candy canes hanging on it, make sure you tell whoever owns the tree what those candy canes mean.

John 15:9-11

Balloon-head

THEME: When we fill ourselves with worldly things, they don't last. Only Christ can fill us with permanent joy.
SUPPLIES: Some balloons.
POINT: A balloon lets out all its air if it isn't tied. People are like balloons—when we rely on the world for our joy, our joy escapes us; when we look to Christ for our joy, the joy stays.

Do you like balloons? *(Pull out a balloon.)* Me too.
(Inflate a balloon and pause, holding it next to one of your children's faces. Don't tie the balloon yet.)
I think balloons are a lot like people. Let me see you smile.
(Compare children's faces and your balloon.)
Yes. Definitely. Your shiny, happy faces are just like this shiny, full balloon. When we're full of joy, we look like a full balloon.
(Let the air out of the balloon.)
Let me try something else. Can I see your sad faces?
(Urge the children to frown and compare the deflated balloon with their faces.)
Oh, for sure. Your droopy, sad faces are just like this droopy, flat balloon. When all of our happiness is gone,

we look deflated and droopy.

(Inflate the balloon again without tying it.)

In our lives there are lots of things that make us happy: toys, candy, food, money, success, friends and families. But as our life goes on, we'll realize that these things don't last; and when we fill ourselves up with these things, our happiness doesn't last. And do you know what that means?

(Release the balloon and let it fly around as the air escapes. When it's done deflating, hold up the droopy balloon.)

When the things that make us happy go away, so does our happiness.

(Begin inflating balloon again.)

Now it doesn't make much sense to fill ourselves up with things that don't last, does it? Why not?

(Let the children respond and then release the balloon again.)

But there is something, or someone, the Bible tells us will never go away.

(Inflate balloon one last time and tie it.)

And if we let him fill us up with our joy—if we put our trust in him—then our joy will never go away.

(Release balloon and let it bounce to the floor.)

That someone is Jesus Christ, and if we want to have real joy, the kind that lasts forever, then we need to fill up with him.

John 14:6

Heavenly Packing

THEME: Jesus is the only way to get to heaven.
SUPPLIES: Suitcase, sunglasses, toothpaste/toothbrush, boxer shorts, socks, suntan lotion, swimming suit, Kleenex, clipboard, paper and pen.
POINT: It doesn't matter what you take to heaven, you won't get there unless you've packed Jesus.

Are you excited about going to heaven? I am. I'm so excited I've already started packing.

(Haul out suitcase and open it.)

Let's see *(check off items on your clipboard as you pull them out of your suitcase).*

- Toothbrush/toothpaste - Check.
- Extra underwear - Check.
- Socks - Check.

- Sunglasses - Check. It's going to be bright up there with all the gold and precious stones.
- Suntan lotion - Check. It's like day all the time there.
- Kleenex - Hey, how did this get in here? There is no crying in heaven so I won't need this.

- Swimming Suit - Check.
- Golf Clubs - Check. They're in the car.

Wait a minute. There's something I'm missing. Oh, this always happens when I pack for a trip. I feel like I'm forgetting something. What am I forgetting?

Of course! I'm forgetting the most important thing— Jesus. You see, without Jesus, you can't get to heaven. Jesus said, "I am the way and the truth and the life. No one comes to the Father [who is in heaven] except through me" (John 14:6).

Now, we all know that there is no sin in heaven, so we need Jesus to take away our sins so that we can go to heaven and be with God. And Jesus can only take away our sins and come and live in our hearts if we say that we're sorry for our sin. I hope that you have Jesus packed in your hearts and if you don't, I hope you get him soon because I sure would like to see you there in heaven.

Matthew 6:31-34

Is It Cold in Here?

THEME: Don't worry, God cares for all of our needs.
SUPPLIES: Piece of paper bearing the above verses, scarf, mittens, winter coat and hat.
POINT: This story illustrates the love-filled provision of God for his people.

(Before you do this story, hide the paper, mittens, scarf and hat in the pockets and sleeves of the coat. Have the coat ready near the front.)
I'm a little unprepared today, so you'll have to bear with me. I've been worrying all morning because I don't have a children's story prepared for you this morning. *(Act like you really don't have anything to say—look around the room, scratch your head.)* So . . . um . . . is it cold in here or is it just me? *(Fake a shiver, rub your arms and blow on your hands.)*
I feel a bit bad that I haven't got a story ready for you, but I . . . boy, I'm really cold. *(Stand up and look around the room for the coat you have waiting. When you see it, act*

as though it isn't yours.) Hey, is this somebody's coat? I'm just going to put this on while I spend a couple of moments here with you children. *(Put on the coat but keep the rest of the items hidden for now.)*

Hmm. My ears still feel a little cold. I wonder if there is anything else. *(While you're talking, pat the pockets of the coat as though you are searching for something else.)* Hey! Here's a hat. *(Produce the hat and put it on.)* Great. *(Blow on your hands, then act as if you have an idea. Check the pockets of the coat—mittens! Put them on.)* Wow, this is a great coat. It has everything I need. Why, I bet it even has a scarf! *(Pull the scarf out of your sleeve, or wherever you've hidden it. Put on the scarf.)*

This is super. I'm feeling a lot warmer now. I guess this coat would really be perfect if it could come up with a children's story idea for me too. I really feel bad, I don't even have a Bible verse this morning. *(Put your hands in the pockets of the coat and try to look a bit embarrassed.)*

Wait a minute. *(Move your hand around in the pocket with the piece of paper.)* What's this? *(Pull out the paper and read it aloud.)* Matthew 6:31-34. It's Bible verses! *(Grab a Bible, look up the verses and read them to the children.)*

That's true, isn't it? God gives us everything we need. He doesn't want us to be hungry, cold or worried; but most of all, he doesn't want us to be slaves to sin. That's why he has given us Jesus. Wow! Do you know what? *(Look at the coat and accessories you're wearing.)* I think God has given us a children's story today too! Let's thank him for all he provides. *(Pray.)*

Luke 18:20

My Own Miracle

THEME: Mothers are miracles sent to us from God.
SUPPLIES: Marker, paper with the letters "M O M."
POINT: A mother loves like God does, unconditionally, and mothers deserve our praise and respect.

Whose special day is today? Right, it's Mother's Day. You love your mothers, don't you? I love mine too. You know our mothers are very special people. Do you know why? Well, it's in their name actually.

You see mom *(show the paper with the word "MOM" on it)* is an abbreviation for *(write it out as you say it)* "My Own Miracle."

Our moms are our very own miracles sent to us from God. Our moms are miraculous because, well, they put up with us.

Did you know that our moms love us no matter what? That's a miracle, and that's the kind of love that only God can give to someone—to be able to love a person no matter what. That's the way God loves us. I'd say that our moms deserve a lot of praise and respect, and at the least we should love them back.

Today, Mother's Day, is the day we celebrate our moms, and we need to try extra hard to please our moms today. You know we do a lot of things that disappoint our moms: we disobey them, or say unkind things, or make a mess. Sometimes we play too rough and too loud. Today, we really need to be aware of when we might be acting in a disappointing way.

Now, I have a fair bit of experience with moms, so I've

prepared a short list of warning signs for you to use so that you will know when your mom may be getting to the point when she needs you to settle down.

- She calls you by your full name—"Zachary David Hapeman!" OK, this is a classic warning sign. You may want to tone things down a little when you hear this.

- Instead of using your name, your mom refers to you as "Young man!" or "Young lady!" Another classic warning sign. This may be accompanied by a tapping foot or crossed arms. *(Demonstrate.)* Body language is important, so pay attention to everything.

- She uses the phrase "I'm going to tell your father!" By this point you may have pushed things too far. Enact immediate countermeasures.

- A pinched ear followed by the words: "That's it! You're coming with me!" A variation of this is called the "elbow dangle." *(Demonstrate how a child might look being quickly pulled along by the elbow.)* At this point I'd say you've probably blown it and you're in big trouble.

Now it may happen that you encounter a combination of these warning signs. *(Demonstrate the four signs and their variations in rapid succession.)* Zachary David Hapeman! Young man! I'm going to tell your father!" *(Pinched ear.)* "That's it!" *(Demonstrate elbow dangle.)* "You're coming with me!"

In the extreme event that you experience a combo like this, well, heaven help you.

Now the point of all this is that we need to try our best to please our moms, not disappoint them, because our moms are very precious. Let's all promise each other to treat our moms like precious people, OK? All right! Now let's thank God for our moms. *(Pray.)*

John 10:14, 15

Golf Ball Savior

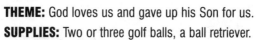

THEME: God loves us and gave up his Son for us.
SUPPLIES: Two or three golf balls, a ball retriever.
POINT: Demonstrating the function of the ball retriever (saving golf balls) will illustrate God's reason for sending Jesus to earth.

You know I love the game of golf. There's only one problem: I'm not very good at it.

When you're not very good at golf, these *(golf balls)* become very precious to you. Golf balls become very precious because when you're not very good at golf, you hit these in some very strange places and tend to lose a lot of them.

Sometimes I lose balls in the woods, sometimes I lose them in tall grass, but most times I lose them in the water. When I lose them in the water, it's especially bad because those are the ones I can't go get. You see, if I hit a ball in the woods, I can go look for it, but when I hit it in the water, that precious little ball is lost.

So that's why I got one of these *(produce ball retriever)*. Now when I lose one of my precious golf balls in the water, I can save it with my ball retriever.

(Extend ball retriever to full length and demonstrate with a ball how you can retrieve it.)

I love my ball retriever, but I think my golf balls love it more, because it keeps us together and those precious little balls can be used the way they are supposed to be used, to play golf.

I want you to remember that just like these golf balls, you are precious. God loves you very much.

Unfortunately, we have all fallen into a deep pool of sin, just like these golf balls that have fallen into the water. Sin separates us from God; it keeps us from being with him.

But let's thank God because he loves each of us so much, he has figured out a way to reach down and save us from sin. God sent Jesus to free us from sin. Jesus saves us from sin just like my ball retriever saves my golf balls, but Jesus is much more than this ball retriever. Jesus is a person, and he loves us as much as God does and he wants to be our friend. Now I like this golf ball retriever, but it sure isn't much like a friend or even a person.

Let's thank God for sending Jesus to save us, and let's thank Jesus for being our friend. *(Pray.)*

Mark 10:19

Dad's Baby Born

THEME: Father's Day is a good time to thank God for fathers.
SUPPLIES: A small mirror.
POINT: Although dads like to build things to be proud of, the things they've made that they're most proud of is their children.

(Keep the mirror hidden until it is used in the story.) As I'm sure you know, today is Father's Day. That means it's a good day to thank God for dads.

Dads are interesting people, aren't they? Dads like to build stuff. Some dads build cars, some build furniture, some even build their houses. Can you tell me what your dad likes to build?

When dads build things, they're awfully proud of those things, aren't they? They like to sit down with their feet up and look at that beautiful new whatchamacallit. They'll spend hours just admiring it and talking about their new creation. Yes, we have to agree that dads are interesting people indeed.

But do you know, of all the things your dad has made, which thing he is most proud of? *(Let the children take a few guesses; they might even get it.)* Well, I have what your dad is most proud of right here. Would you like to see what it is? *(Produce the mirror and face it toward the children so they can see themselves.)*

Your dad is most proud of you. You are the closest he is ever going to get to making something that is perfect. Dads love the things they make, but the one thing they love most of all is their children. Now there is nothing strange about that, is there?

Let's make a promise today to be good for our dads and our heavenly Father, God. The Bible has given us the commandment that we should honor our mother and father and the Bible also tells us that a good son or daughter brings "great joy" to his or her father (Proverbs 23:24). So let's make a pact together, OK?

Please raise your right hand and repeat after me:

(This is meant to start serious, get silly and end serious again, so if you lose the children for a bit, don't worry; it's all in good fun.)

I promise . . .
to be good for my dad . . .
And . . .
I pledge . . .
All of my mental, emotional and physical faculties . . .
To treating dad with love . . .
And I . . .

Insert your name here . . . *(gets them every time)*
will never . . .

Never, never . . .

No not ever . . .

Willfully attempt to damage the aforementioned paternal unit . . .

And . . .

I will love . . .

My dad . . .

And thank God for him . . .

As long as I live.

(Open your mouth as if to say "and" again and you'll get a good groan from everyone.)

(Pray.)

Matthew 5:8

Heart Wash

THEME: Jesus is the only one who can purify our hearts.

SUPPLIES: Bar of soap, washcloth, bowl of water and a hand towel.

POINT: The children will see that we can't purify our hearts on our own; we need Jesus to do it for us.

Isn't it a lovely day? I have been reading my Bible and I found a verse that is very interesting. It says: *(Read Matthew 5:8 aloud)*. That means that if we have pure hearts, we can be with God. Now a pure heart is one that is totally clean and without sin, so I brought everything we need to have pure/clean hearts here this morning.

(Lather up the washcloth with the soap and water.)

All right. Who wants to be first?

(Hopefully the children will be a bit confused. After all, how can you clean a heart? You may, however, get a volunteer or two. That's fine, they'll get the point shortly.)

Anyone? OK, all I need are your hearts. Give me your heart and I will clean it up for you. *(The bafflement should be readily at hand now.)* Doesn't anyone want a pure heart? Just hand over your heart and I will make it pure for you.

Well, this isn't going to work, is it? Why can't I clean any of your hearts? *(Let the children respond.)* I can't clean your hearts because I can't even see your hearts, let alone get my hands on them. Who can see our hearts? *(Let them respond again.)* That's right, God can see our hearts. So he would be the perfect one to clean our hearts, to make them pure, right?

Does God use soap and water to purify our hearts? No, he uses Jesus Christ. Jesus died on the cross so that our sinful, dirty hearts could be pure like his. Now all we have to do is give our hearts to him to be cleaned. The Bible tells us that if we believe in Jesus, and we tell him we're sorry for our sins, he will take our hearts and purify them (1 John 1:9).

And once our hearts have been purified, we're on our way to see God. Let's thank him for all his goodness. *(Pray.)*

Matthew 6:19-21

Treasure Chests

THEME: Make sure your heart is with God, or you'll get burned.

SUPPLIES: Three heart-shaped cut-outs (two crumpled, torn and maybe even slightly burned), a Bible and two of your favorite earthly things. (I used a set of golf clubs and an old bag of potato chips.)

POINT: Children will see that the hearts you have placed with your earthly favorite things are destroyed, while the heart you have placed in your Bible is like new.

(When you prepare for this story, put the two damaged hearts with your earthly favorites and your good heart in your Bible.)

I have brought some of my favorite things to show you today. These are things I treasure very much, and I have put my heart into these things because I love them so.

First—potato chips! I love potato chips. *(Show the children the bag which has already been opened and contains your heart inside. Pull out a chip and eat it.)* These are my favorite snack—ugh. These have gone stale. I can't eat them. Boy they sure didn't last long. Wow. That's disappointing. I really put my heart into potato chips and *(pull the damaged heart out of the bag)*—my heart! Well, that's too bad.

I brought another of my favorite things—my golf clubs. *(Produce your clubs from their hiding spot.)* Now this is something I can really put my heart into. Let's see . . . boy, they sure are dirty. I'll show you my favorite club, it's my seven iron and I always hit a good shot with . . . where is my seven iron? It's not here. I must have lost it. Maybe it got stolen. Oh no! My seven iron is gone, that's really sad . . . *(pull out your second damaged heart)*—my heart! Gee, I wish I hadn't lost that club.

Well, I've got one more favorite thing to show you *(act dejectedly as though you are expecting the worst for this as well)*. I want to read you one of my favorite Bible passages *(pull out your Bible)*. The passage comes from Matthew chapter 6, verses 19 to 21. *(Read the passage aloud slowly and change the text if you feel the children will understand it better if it is worded a little differently. I read it like this: "Don't put your heart into things of the earth, where it can get ruined or stolen. Instead, put your heart into the things of heaven, where it will last forever. For your heart and your treasure are always together." Once you've read the passage, pull out the good heart from the Bible.)*

Wow, look at that! My heart looks great. I guess when you put your heart into the things of God, he keeps it safe and makes sure it lasts. I hope you put your hearts in heaven. Let's pray.

The super Deluxe Mountain Relocation Device

THEME: With faith and God all things are possible.

SUPPLIES: A big box (I used a refrigerator box) and a mustard seed.

POINT: The contrast between the large box and the tiny mustard seed will help children recognize the significance of faith and the power of God to do the impossible.

(If you want, tape the mustard seed to the inside of the box so you don't lose it.)

I bet you're wondering what's inside this big box. It must be something really important to demand such a large box. Well, let me tell you that inside this box are the tools to make the impossible possible. The thing in this box can move a mountain, it can cut a sea in half, it can feed thousands of people, and it can change the world.

Do you want to see it? Are you sure you want to see it? It's quite thrilling. OK. *(Open the box and let the children peer inside but they probably won't see the mustard seed. After they've all had opportunity to look, reach in and pull out the mustard seed.)*

There it is. The thing that makes the impossible

possible—a mustard seed. My knees are quaking just looking at it. How about you? *(The children should be quite confused, maybe even a bit disappointed.)*

Jesus said that if we have a faith even as small as a mustard seed—if we just believe this much *(point to the seed)* that God can do the impossible—then anything is possible, absolutely anything. Imagine, if we had a whole finger full of faith, or a whole body full, or a whole church full of faith, what would be possible? Let's ask God to give us the faith to make the impossible possible. *(Pray.)*

Matthew 4:4

Technology Theology

THEME: In the age of information, the Word of God is still our best source of knowledge.

SUPPLIES: An overhead projector, a wall or screen for projections, three transparencies (or one cut into three pieces), a computer keyboard and an assistant.

POINT: As questions about healthy living are typed on the keyboard, the projection screen will show the answers in Scripture. The children will see that the Bible is the processor powering all of these answers and it is our best source of information.

(Try to keep your assistant and the overhead projector hidden from the children. Make sure your assistant has three transparencies bearing the following Scripture verses: Matthew 4:4; Deuteronomy 31:8; Luke 6:27-31. Stash the keyboard ahead of time in your children's area and have the keyboard

cord resting inside a closed Bible which is hidden from view or at least behind you.)

Today I have a special treat for you—the world's greatest computer. This processor can answer any question about living a happy and fulfilling life, and it is powered by the world's most advanced technology. Let's try it out, shall we?

Sometimes we feel lonely, don't we? Well let's see what our super computer has to say about loneliness.

(Type the word "loneliness" on the keyboard—get the children to help you if you like—and have your hidden assistant display Deuteronomy 31:8 on the projection screen. Read the verse aloud.)

Wow! So God is always with us and we are never really alone. Let's ask the computer something else. We all know people that we don't get along with very well. Let's ask the computer what we should do with our enemies, and those people we don't like.

(Type in the word "enemies" and repeat the process above. This time your assistant should project Luke 6:27-31. Read the verses aloud.)

That's pretty good advice for us as Christians; after all, it's the example Jesus set for us. You know, I've always wanted to know what it is we really need to live healthy Christian lives. Let's ask the computer.

(This time type the word "healthy" on your keyboard and have your assistant show Matthew 4:4 on the screen. Read the verse aloud.)

That's really true. We need God's guidance to live properly and to be more like Christ. This is a great computer, isn't it? I wonder what the processor looks like, I mean, what kind of brain it has. *(Follow the keyboard cord to the hidden Bible.)*

Look, this computer is powered by the Bible. I should have known that the brain behind these answers was God's. Do any of you have a super computer like this at your house *(referring to the Bible)*? Why don't we thank God for giving us such great technical support. *(Pray.)*

John 17:22, 23

Body parts

THEME: God desires that we work together as one.

SUPPLIES: Paper cutouts of body parts for every child you expect to have (legs, arms, hands, torsos, feet and heads; crosses on heads only); enough envelopes to hold each individual body part; tape.

POINT: The children will learn that God wants us to be parts of a body of people, using our gifts together under Christ's leadership and for his glory.

(Having put all the body parts into individual envelopes, keep the envelopes with the heads in your pocket.)

I have a special gift for each of you today. These gifts come from God. *(Hand out envelopes to every child but keep the heads in your pocket.)*

Well, open them! Let's see what you got.

(Let the children open their envelopes and ask them what they received.)

Wow, you got an arm. And look at you, you've got a foot. Did anyone get a hand? Great!

These are super gifts but wouldn't they be even better if we put them together?

(One-by-one ask children to contribute their gifts to be connected appropriately to a body as it grows. Make more than one body if you have that many children.)

You know, these paper body parts are like the gifts God has given us. Some of us are good at cleaning, some of us are good at building houses, some of us are good at speaking, and some are good at teaching. All of these are things God has given to us and he wants us to use them together as a body of people in a church. Together, as a body of believers who all have different gifts, we become a church that isn't a building but a group of people.

(By now, the children should be commenting that your body is headless.)

What is our body missing? *(The head.)*

Right! This body needs a head. *(Pull out the head and attach it to the body.)*

Now what's different about this body part? *(The cross.)*

Yes, this head has a cross on it. That's because the head of this body is Jesus. The Bible tells us that Jesus is supposed to be the head of the church. He knows exactly where and when the other body parts should be used; so all the other body parts are guided by the head, just as we, the people in this church, look for guidance from Jesus.

(Give away the body your group has made if you can do so without causing trouble.)

Let's thank God for our gifts and ask him to help us use them together with Christ as the head. *(Pray.)*

John 13:34

Let Me Be Your Elbows

THEME: Being a loving person makes life so much easier.

SUPPLIES: Four sticks about a foot and a half long, some masking tape, and two pieces of fruit.

POINT: Two volunteers will be unable to feed themselves because of the sticks taped to their arms. Only when they help each other will they be fed.

Have you ever thought about how important elbows are? We need our elbows, don't we? Well I need two volunteers who like grapes to come and help me for a minute. *(Make sure the volunteers have long sleeves.)*

I would like to show you how important our elbows are, but more importantly, I want to show you how important helping each other is. OK, now I need both of my volunteers to stand with their arms very straight while I attach their elbow disabling units.

(Place a stick against the arm of your volunteer and run a piece of masking tape around the stick and arm at the top, middle, and bottom of the stick. Repeat this for both arms on each of your volunteers. Make sure the tape is stuck to the shirt sleeves of your volunteers and not their skin.)

All right, now I have some grapes here *(bring out the grapes or other fruit you have brought)* that I want you to eat. *(Put a grape in the hand of each of your volunteers.)* Now, I know how much each of you like grapes, so go ahead and eat them.

(Your volunteers will be struggling with trying to get the grape to their mouths. Let them try for half a minute; it can be comical to watch.)

It's not so easy to eat without your elbows, is it? Well, let's pretend that you haven't eaten for two or three days, that you're really hungry, and all there is to eat are these grapes. You don't want to drop them on the floor because it's covered with dead bugs and hair and fuzz *(no offense to the janitor)*. So how are you two going to eat? You're starving!

(The children might figure it out: they can eat if they feed each other. If they don't discover this solution, offer it as a suggestion to them.)

Well, what would happen if you decided that you couldn't eat because you can't bend your elbows, but you could act as each other's elbows. In other words, you could feed each other. The Bible gives us a commandment that says: "Love one another." One of the best ways we can love each other is by helping each other, by becoming elbows for other people. There are lots of things people need help with and God has prepared us especially to become elbows for people who need help.

I'm sure you could all think of people who have acted

as elbows for you, but one person who has really been a help to us is God. He sent his Son, Jesus, to free us from sin. Let's thank him for all his help. *(Pray.)*